A BEACON BIOGRAPHY

Oprah Winfrey

Tamra B. Orr

PURPLE TOAD
PUBLISHING

PURPLE TOAD
PUBLISHING

Printing   1   2   3   4   5   6   7   8   9

A Beacon Biography

Library of Congress Cataloging-in-Publication Data
Orr, Tamra B.
   Oprah Winfrey / Written by Tamra B. Orr.
     p. cm.
Includes bibliographic, references, glossary, and index.
ISBN 9781624694288
1. Winfrey, Oprah. 1954—Juvenile literature. 2. Television Personalities—United States—Biography —Juvenile literature. 3. Actors—African American Female—Juvenile literature. I. Series: A Beacon Biography
 PN1992.4.W56A45 2019
 791.4502
[B]
                                                        Library of Congress Control Number: 2018943801
eBook ISBN: 9781624694271

ABOUT THE AUTHOR: Tamra B. Orr is a full-time author living in the Pacific Northwest with her family. She graduated from Ball State University in Muncie, Indiana. She has written more than 500 books about everything from historical events and career choices to controversial issues and celebrity biographies. On those rare occasions that she is not writing a book, she is reading one. She has watched countless episodes of *Oprah*, is an Oprah Book Club member, and is grateful for the opportunity to learn more about one of her role models.

PUBLISHER'S NOTE: This story has not been authorized or endorsed by Oprah Winfrey.

CONTENTS

*Oprah celebrates her
50th birthday in style.*

A Rainbow in the Clouds

It was a very dark time for the young teenager. In many ways, it felt like her life was falling apart. She needed help but did not know where to turn. And then she found an unexpected lifeline in the words of a book.

For the first time in her life, young Oprah Winfrey read books and poems by an author to whom she could truly relate. She connected powerfully with the words in Maya Angelou's autobiography, *I Know Why the Caged Bird Sings*. "I read it over and over," she stated to Thought.co. "I had never before read a book that validated my own existence." Both Angelou and Winfrey had grown up in very similar ways, suffering some of the same tragedies, and learning some of the same survival skills. Angelou had gone on to become one of the world's most beloved figures. This gave young Winfrey hope—and inspiration.

Many years later, she wrote in her magazine *O*, "With each page, [Angelou's] life seemed to mirror mine. . . . Meeting Maya on those pages was like meeting myself in full. For the first time, as a young black girl, my experience was validated."

Maya Angelou was one of literature's most beloved poets and authors. She spoke at many gatherings and special events.

Although Maya Angelou wrote about her life in seven books, most people are familiar with *I Know Why the Caged Bird Sings*. The book covers the author's earlier years, from the early 1930s to 1970. It inspired many other writers to share their life stories—and it certainly inspired teenage Oprah, who needed guidance at a low point in her life.

Long after Oprah became famous, she met Maya Angelou in person. The two became instant close friends. Not only did Oprah interview her role model multiple times, but they also spent time together in their personal lives. When the anniversary edition of *I Know Why the Caged Bird Sings* was issued, Random House asked Oprah to write the foreword to it. She wrote, "Maya Angelou lived what she wrote. She understands that sharing her truth connected her to the greater human truths—of longing, abandonment, security, hope,

wonder, prejudice, mystery, and finally self-discovery: the realization of who you really are and the liberation that love brings."

In May 2014, Maya Angelou died. Oprah spoke at her funeral. "She was there for me always, guiding me through some of the most important years of my life," she stated. "The world knows her as a poet, but at the heart of her, she was a teacher. 'When you learn, teach. When you get, give' is one of my best lessons from her. She moved through the world with unshakeable calm, confidence, and a fierce grace. I loved her and I know she loved me. I will profoundly miss her. She will always be the rainbow in my clouds."

Today, Oprah's name is familiar around the world. She is known for her thoughtful interviews, her strong opinions, her generosity, and her passion for giving. Long before that, however, she had to endure a difficult childhood—and obstacles that would have her searching for that rainbow in the clouds.

Oprah's smile is a familiar sight to most people, but, for many years, smiles were hard to find for the young woman.

shadrach
meshach
abednego
jeremiah
nehemiah
deuteronomy
leviticus
hippopotamus
elephant

Speaking at "The Life You Want" summit in New York City, Oprah showed where she had started— and how far she had come.

The world came very close to not having an Oprah—but an Orpah.
When she was born on January 29, 1954, in the small farming
community of Kosciusko [kah-SHOO-skoh], Mississippi, her parents
called her Orpah Gail. The name Orpah comes from the Hebrew
Bible's Book of Ruth. However, it was hard to say and harder to spell.
People started to call her Oprah, and they kept spelling it that way, too.

Oprah's father was 20-year-old Vernon Winfrey, a sometimes
barber. Her mother was 18-year-old Vernita Lee. The two were not
married, and having a baby did not bring them any closer together. It
was not long before both of them went their own way, leaving baby
Oprah on the farm with her grandmother, Hattie Mae Lee. Hattie was
quite strict and focused on making sure Oprah did her chores, went to
school, and attended church. She believed in physical discipline, and
sometimes enforced her lessons with a harsh slap or smack.

Cheese grits was one of the most common dishes on grandmother's table.

Despite this, Oprah still has some wonderful memories of her grandmother. She used to help her cook. In the introduction to the cookbook *In the Kitchen with Rosie*, Oprah writes, "I grew up eating well. Cheese grits, homemade biscuits smothered in butter, home-cured ham, red-eyed gravy—and that was just breakfast. Smothered chicken, butter beans, fried corn, and corn bread was a typical weekday dinner," she added. "Food was the guest of honor, covering so much of the table there was hardly room for plates." Over time, Oprah associated food with security and comfort. "Food meant love," she wrote. "It didn't matter what you ate, just that you had enough." This way of thinking would cause her problems later in life. As she put it, "I've paid a heavy price for believing that. It took me a long time to change the way I thought about food."

By the age of three, Oprah had learned to read. She commonly performed her own stories to the animals on the farm. She also recited Bible verses she had memorized to the congregation at her grandmother's church. Oprah quickly realized that talking in front of people and keeping them entertained was fun. She wanted to keep doing it.

Because she was able to read so young, Oprah skipped kindergarten and started first grade at the age of six. She did so well, she was also able to skip second grade. Despite her success in school, home life was hard. She was taken away from the farm to live with her mother and father—but not at the same time. She often moved back and forth between a boarding house in Milwaukee with her mother and an apartment in Nashville, Tennessee, with her father and his new family.

For the next four years, Oprah's life was difficult. Living with her mother was lonely. Vernita worked long hours as a maid, and Oprah was left on her own quite a lot. Her 19-year-old cousin sometimes babysat, but that only made life much harder because the teen was sexually abusing Oprah. So were others. "I was raped at nine years old by a cousin, then again by another family member, and then another family member," she revealed on her show in 1986. "I know what it feels like to be abandoned," she stated in a PBS documentary, *Makers: Women Who Make America*. "I know what it feels like to not be wanted. I know what it feels like to not be loved . . . and yet have inside yourself a yearning, a passion, a desire, a *hope* for something better."

At age 14, Oprah was given a scholarship to attend Nicolet High School in Glendale, Wisconsin. It sounded like a great direction, but trouble was waiting just ahead. Still living with her mother, Oprah was stealing money and skipping school. In 1968, she ran away. She "started running in the streets," she stated in the *Makers* documentary. And then . . . life got ever harder.

Nicolet High School was a chance for Oprah to excel, but it would not be easy.

Oprah arrives at the University of the Free in Free State, South Africa, to receive an honorary degree for her work in promoting education.

Hitting
Rock Bottom

At the age of 14, Oprah found herself pregnant. "I hid the pregnancy until literally the day the child was born," she stated in *Makers*. The baby boy was born too early and died two weeks later. "When this baby died," Oprah added, "my father said to me, 'This is your second chance.'"

"I hit rock-bottom," Oprah told *Hollywood Reporter*. She seriously considered suicide. Instead, she went to live with her father, and that helped her turn around. Like Hattie Mae, he was strict, but his focus was on education. Oprah was expected to write weekly book reports to turn in to him, and if she hadn't learned five new vocabulary words in a day, she did not get any dinner. "As strict as he was," Oprah told Achievement.org, "he had some concerns about me making the best of my life, and would not accept anything less than what he thought was my best." She added in an interview on *Learning LiftOff*, "My father turned my life around by insisting that I be more than I was. His love of learning showed me the way."

Poet Angelou was inspired by African-American poet Paul Laurence Dunbar (above). He wrote about the caged bird as a symbol for the chained slave.

And then, Oprah picked up *I Know Why the Caged Bird Sings*. She found out she was not alone in all that she had experienced. "In [Angelou's] early years, she was raised by her grandmother in the South; as a young girl she was raped," Oprah wrote in her magazine. "When you see other people who have come through the worst, survived what you're going through, that lets you know you can," she added in *Maker*.

In 1970, Oprah put all of her energy and time into her education. By the time she was a senior in East Nashville High School, she had won a local speech contest and a four-year scholarship to Tennessee State University (TSU). She was an honors student and was voted Most Popular Girl. She was crowned Miss Fire Prevention by WVOL, a local radio station. They were so impressed by her, the station hired her to read afternoon newscasts. Oprah was on the air!

At TSU, Oprah focused on getting a degree in radio and TV broadcasting. In 1972, she was also named Miss Black Nashville and Miss Tennessee. The next year, Oprah graduated from TSU with a degree in Speech and Performing Arts. She was hired as the first black television news anchor with WTVF-TV.

In 1976, she moved to Baltimore to be on the six o'clock news. From there, she went on to host a local talk show, *People Are Talking*. It was a huge hit. Clearly Oprah was destined to be in the spotlight, but she could never have imagined what was ahead.

From the time she recited Bible verses in church, Oprah knew that she wanted to spend her life talking to people—a goal she certainly fulfilled.

Part of what makes Oprah's interviews unique is that she travels to people's homes to speak with them, as she does here with Justin Bieber.

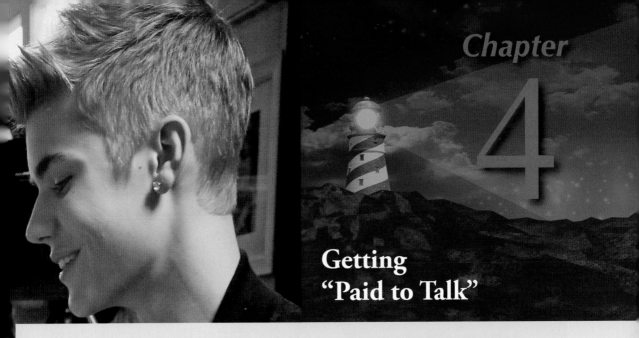

Getting "Paid to Talk"

Ever since Oprah had told her stories to the farm animals, she knew that performing was fun. When she won the speech contests, she realized she could be paid for talking. Now she was going to make it her career.

In 1984, Oprah moved to Chicago to host a 30-minute morning show called *AM Chicago*. Within a month, the show went from the lowest ratings to the highest. Within a year, it was expanded to an hour and renamed *The Oprah Winfrey Show*. Along with working on her interviewing skills, Oprah also decided to try acting. She loved the book *The Color Purple* by Alice Walker. The main character, Celie, is abused by her father and then her husband, but the women in the story are strong. "I passed the book around to everybody I knew," she told *Achievement*. "If I was on the bus, I'd pass it out to people. And when I heard that there was going to be a movie, I started talking it up for myself. I didn't know Quincy Jones or Steven Spielberg, or how on Earth I would get in this movie. I'd never acted in my life. But I felt it so intensely that I had to be a part of that movie. I really do believe that I created it for myself. I wanted it more than anything in the world, and would have done anything to do it, anything to do it."

*Steven Spielberg took a risk when he hired two relatively unknown actors to be in **The Color Purple**—Oprah and Whoopie Goldberg.*

She got the part. Steven Spielberg hired her to play Sophia, a friend of Celie's. For this role, she was nominated for an Academy Award for Best Supporting Actress.

A year later, in 1986, Oprah started a new adventure that would propel her to world fame. She started the daily talk show, *The Oprah Winfrey Show*. It ran for 24 seasons, with some 5,000 episodes. It was shown on more than 200 channels in more than 100 countries, and it usually had more than 40 million viewers every week! It won 48 Emmys, and in 1988, Oprah was named Broadcaster of the Year.

That same year, Oprah met the man she would spend most of her adult life with: Stedman Graham. The two met at a charity event, and Oprah was intrigued by the speaker and businessman. The two of them were often photographed together.

Oprah's career soared. In 1988, she established her own television company called Harpo Productions. (*Harpo* is *Oprah* spelled backward.) Harpo has produced shows hosted by such celebrities as Dr. Phil, Rachael Ray, and Dr. Oz. Eleven years later, she cofounded Oxygen Media, a cable TV station with programming for women. She continued to take on special movie and TV miniseries roles, including *Native Son* (1986), *The Women of Brewster Place* (1989), *There Are No*

Children Here (1993), *Before Women Had Wings* (1997), and *Beloved* (1998). In later years, she also provided her voice to animated movies such as *Charlotte's Web*, *The Bee Movie*, and *The Princess and the Frog*.

Oprah never forgot about the abuse she experienced as a child. In 1991, she testified before the U.S. Senate Judiciary Committee to help establish the National Child Protection Act. The act aimed to create a national database of convicted child abusers. "The Oprah Bill," as it was often called, was signed into law by President Bill Clinton in late 1993.

According to People magazine, in 1992, Stedman proposed. "I want you to marry me. I think it's time," he said. "Ah, that's really great," replied Oprah. However, the marriage didn't happen then—or later. In 2017, Oprah admitted to *Vogue* that it wasn't going to. "What I realized is, I don't want to be married," she said. Stedman seems to agree. He told CNN in 2012, "I'm with a very special person who is—she's just so unbelievable but that has nothing to do with my life.

Oprah and Stedman have been together since 1988. He often joins her at special events, such as the oscars in 2015.

19

Stedman is a huge fan of Oprah's projects and supports her in everything she does, including running her own studio.

That's her life. I just support her in her life. And she supports me in my life."

In 1996, in a mission to encourage reading, Oprah launched an international book club. "I'm always on the lookout for stories that offer insights into the African-American journey and struggle and triumph," she told the *Telegraph*.

In addition to recommending a book, and often interviewing the author on her show, she also offers free reading guides and online discussion groups. It did not take long for Oprah's Book Club to become the biggest in the world, with more than two million members. Oprah has written five books herself.

Although success was coming quickly to Oprah, she has had a long struggle with one issue: weight. For years, since those days of cooking with her grandmother, she has tried to lose weight. She has shared her ongoing battle with her millions of television fans. In 2005, she finally reached her ideal weight. "I thought I was finished with the weight battle," she wrote in *O, The Oprah Magazine*. "I was done. I'd conquered it. I was so sure, I was even cocky."

Then, from health problems and a demanding schedule, the weight crept back on. Over the years, Oprah has learned a great deal about the weight battle and what she is truly trying to achieve. "My goal isn't to be thin," she wrote in *O*. "My goal is for my body to be the weight it can hold—to be strong and healthy and fit. My goal is to learn to embrace this body and to be grateful every day for what it has given me." In 2015, she became the official spokesperson for Weight Watchers. Two years later, she published a cookbook called *Food, Health and Happiness.*

Oprah's weight struggle has helped many people all over the world learn that people of any weight can display an elegance all their own. Here she is with **Star Wars** *star Mark Hamill.*

The Leadership Academy for Girls was started by Oprah, with the help and encouragement of Nelson Mandela.

In the first ten years of the twenty-first century, Oprah seemed to be everywhere people looked. She started the magazine *O, The Oprah Magazine*, brought *The Color Purple* to Broadway in New York, and started doing interview specials on evening television. She created the cable company Oprah Winfrey Network (OWN). She opened the Leadership Academy for Girls near Johannesburg, South Africa. At least four times, she travels to check on the students. In 2012, the academy had its first graduating class.

In late 2007, Oprah campaigned for Barack Obama to become U. S. president. She went to many of his rallies. At the University of South Carolina's football stadium, with a crowd of 29,000, she spoke of the possibility of electing the first African American president, "Dr. Martin Luther King dreamed the dream. But we don't have to just dream the dream anymore. We get to vote that deal into reality by supporting a man who knows not just who we are, but who we can be." Many experts believe that Oprah's support helped to secure more than a million votes for Obama.

By this time, Oprah was all over the world. Even though her daily talk show came to an end in 2011, she kept so busy that she barely had a chance to slow down. As she stated on her final show, "This show has been my life. And I love it enough to know when it's time to say goodbye. Twenty-five years feels right in my bones, and it feels right in my spirit. It's the perfect number—the exact right time."

Oprah's support of Barack Obama's run for the U. S. presidency had a strong influence on voters.

In addition to her other charitable works, Oprah also reaches out during natural disasters. In 2014, she visited people who had to flee their homes after Hurricane Katrina devastated New Orleans.